Ben: Thank you to my family and friends for their constant support and a big special thank you to Bjorn Rune Lie, Tom Frost, Alex Spiro, Sam Arthur and lastly, Scott Donaldson for all helping to make this book so much fun to create.

Scott: Thanks muchly to the wife, the dog, the folks, my Untimely brothers, and of course, thanks to Ben for inviting me. I've had a lovely time.

Published by: Nobrow Ltd. 62 Great Eastern Street, London, EC2A 3QR
Typography design by Luke Ngakane

Order from www.nobrow.net
Printed in Belgium on FSC assured paper
ISBN: 978-1-907704-01-7

BY BEN NEWMAN AND SCOTT DONALDSON

NOBROW·PRESS

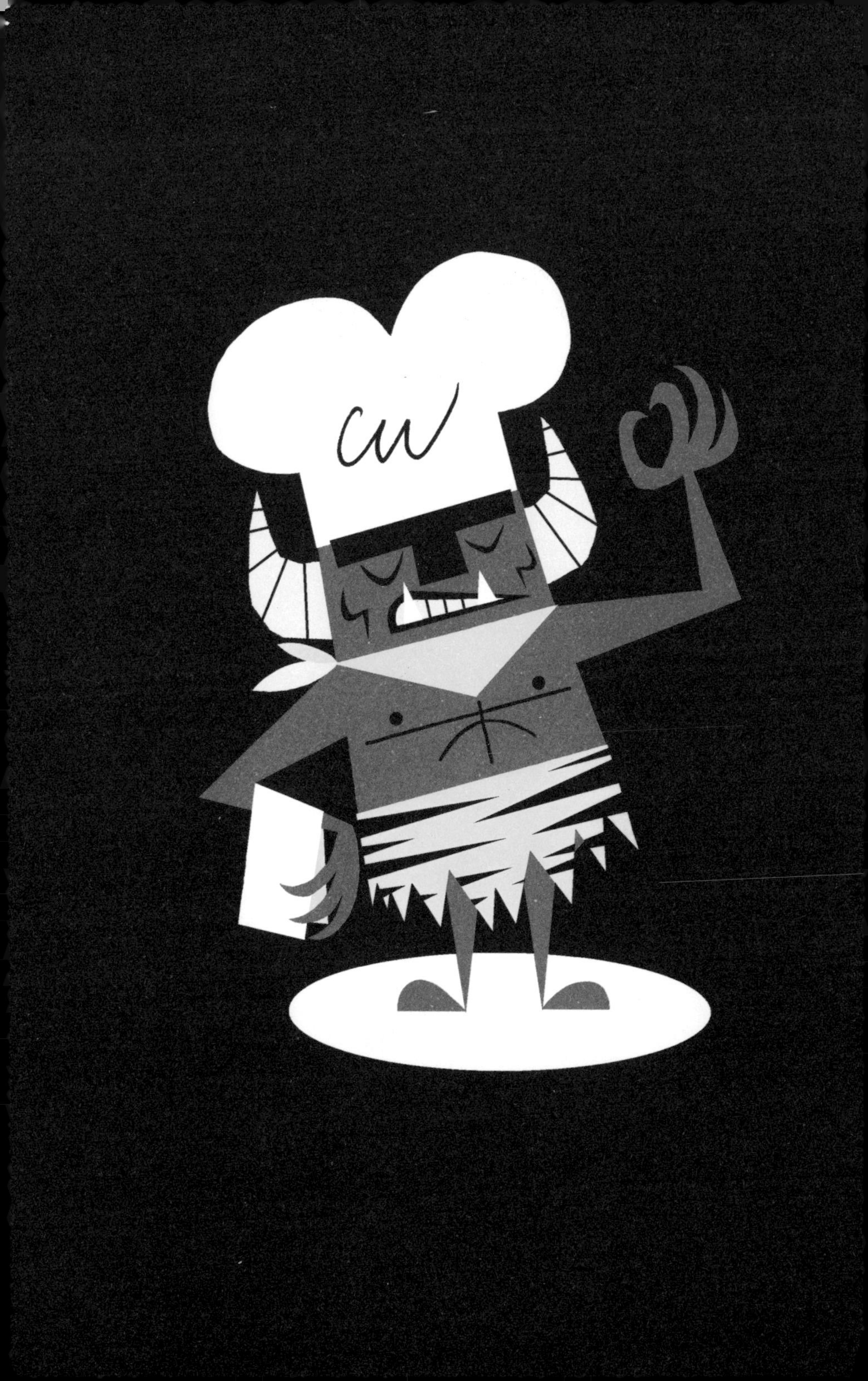

GREETINGS!

And welcome to our lively lunchbox. Here at the Double-B, we take pride in forcing the most throat throttling, the most stomach sickening, and the most bottom burning mythological morsels imaginable down through your tummy-works. Our menu consists of 14 traditional Yokai, and you must tuck into each one or suffer dire consequences.

Now: Sigh with relief as you learn that each bona fide spirit and demon has been resurrected from recipes first set down by 18th Century scholar Toriyama Sekien.

Gasp in wonder when I inform you that we Yokai are not only an underrated source of protein, but that we are also the forefathers of the Kaiju – those famous ugly bugs like Mothra or Godzilla.

Feel your mind pulsate as you learn about our audition process – how the lucky few are hog-tied and shipped to a cramped sweatshop in Bristol. And how, once there, they are pounded and pressed, stir-fried and steamed, then boxed up in Bento, ready for your ingesting pleasure. So come friends. Roll up those trousers or turn up your skirts, and wash your hands and faces.

WE WELCOME YOU, TO THE BENTO BESTIARY.

NINGYO

Endlessly studied by those with nothing better to do, the Ningyo is described as being pleasingly hairier, but no less alluring, than the Western mermaid. Blessed with mythical scales of gold, this really is no ordinary fish. For where the blubbery lips and cold dead eyes common to most sea dwellers would normally perch, we find instead the mischievous mug of a monkey! In fact, it is likely to be this dynamite combination which makes the Ningyo such an excellent flute player.

It would be considered surprisingly rude to catch and eat this creature without first obtaining its written authorisation. If you were to do such a thing, you would most likely die. Or there might be a nasty storm. However – if the legal requirements are met, and you do dine on the aqua-chimp's salty flesh, we are told that you will never grow old, and you will never die.

But where there is magic, misery must follow. Do not forget that everyone you know and love will continue to age and eventually die, leaving you to weep for all eternity, in maddening solitude.

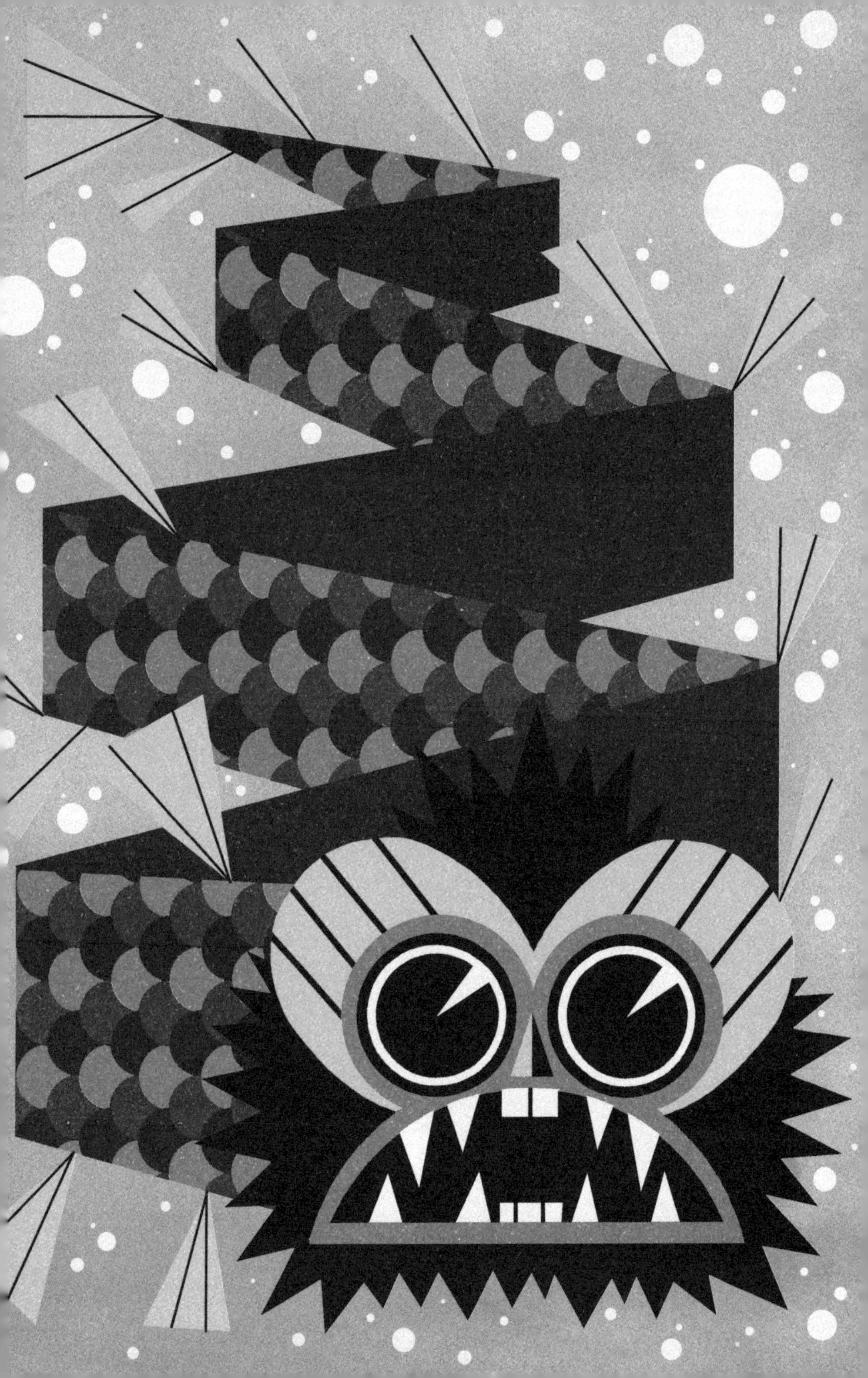

NEKO MATA

If you've ever pondered the inhumanities of spaying your cat, fret no further when I tell you that 9 out of 10 common tabbies will almost probably turn into Neko Mata demons some day. Just picture the scene when, after 13 years of unquestioned love and affection, the beast lying dormant within precious Mr Winkleman can be contained no more, and unimaginable terror bursts forth! With a shriek to bring down the heavens, the creature's tail will split asunder, and all peace will be gone from your life.

NO VETERINARIAN CAN HELP YOU NOW.

No longer content to hunt your tawdry mice, the brute Winkleman will by now be strutting about on hind legs, wearing your finest hats, and raising forth the bodies of the dead, so that they may do his bidding. Before you can say 'Zombo-Apocalypso', your long-gone grandma will be banging the door down demanding your life savings, as well as your soul. Please, try not to be angry with Granny, for she is merely an instrument of the Neko Mata, and before long, you will be too.

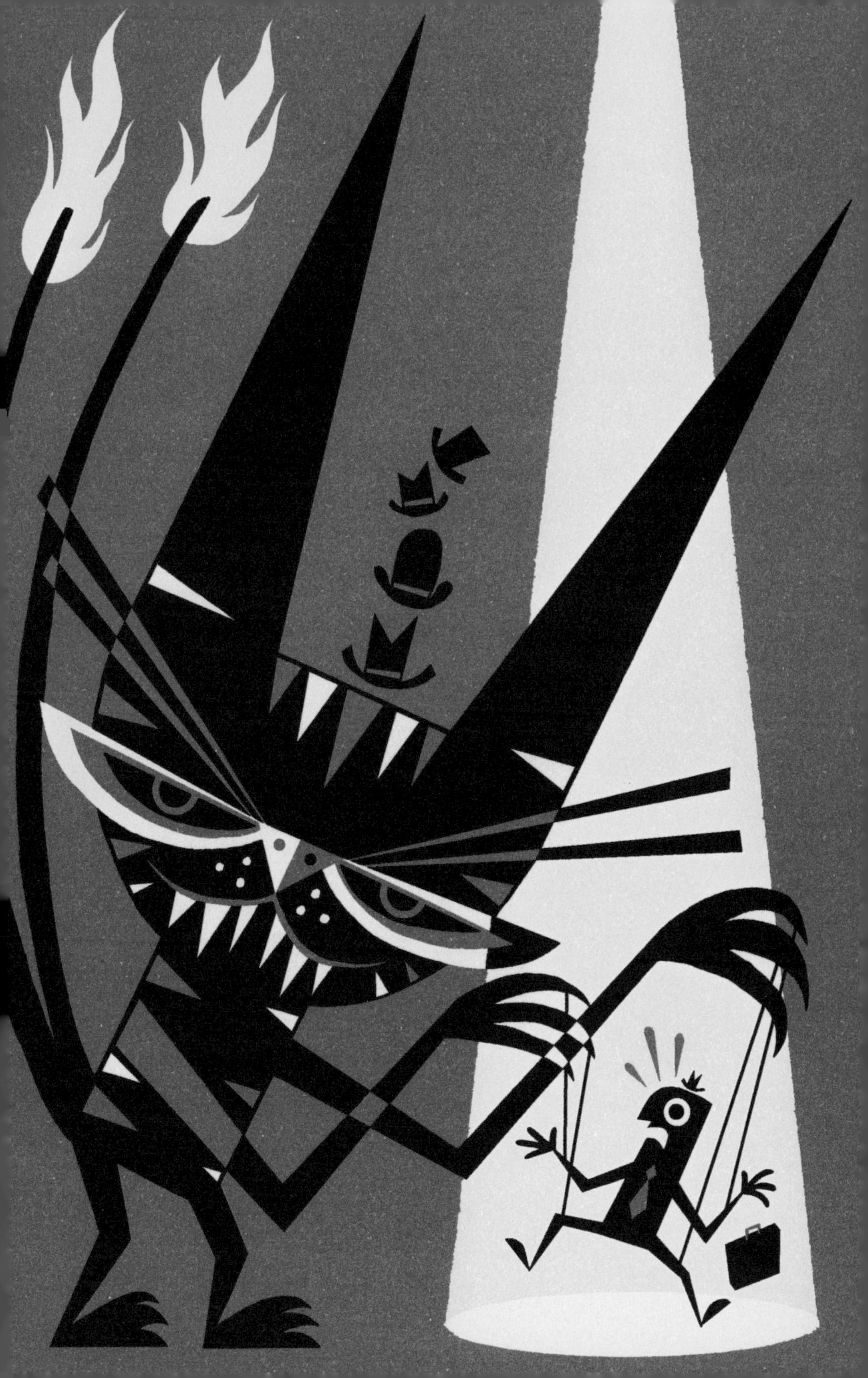

UMIBŌZU

Rub-a-dub-dub, Umibōzu's in the tub! The sea-tub that is! That's right, I live in the ocean, so every night is bath night. Don't worry, it's not as bad as it sounds. I don't have any skin so I never get wrinkly, and I can usually find something to play with, like whales and coral and Ningyo. Sometimes I spot a little fisherman ship and splish-splash I am making the dash straight over there to make friends.

The fishermen always want to play the same game, but I don't mind. First, I'll pop out from under the sea and make the biggest of big waves. Then they'll scream because they are so happy and they'll make their boat move about real quick. Then there's usually some splashing, and I roar with laughter every time. A bit later, they'll normally get tired and go in the sea for a sleep. They get tired pretty easy, but that's ok.

I just wish they could come around more often. It gets so lonely out here sometimes a Yokai could lose his mind.

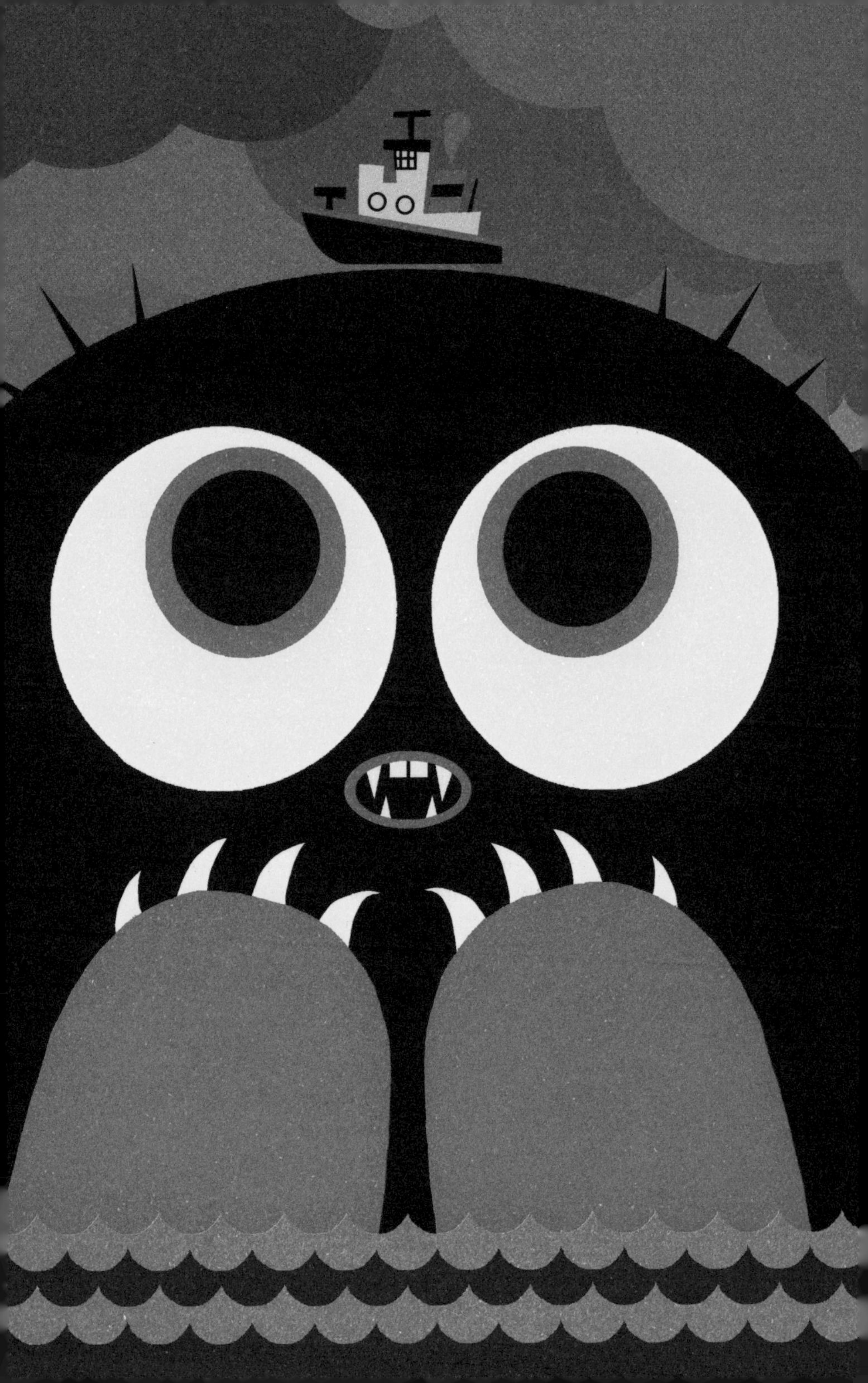

JOROGUMO

PREPARE YOURSELVES!

She'll sing for you. She'll spin for you. She'll commit unspeakable sin for you. Ladies and gentlemen, may I present the world famous Jorogumo!

In the far East, she's called the Silky Siren. In the far West, she's known as the Black-Lace Widow. You can call this eight-legged lovely anything anywhere, as long as you call her Madam first!

FORM AN ORDERLY QUEUE!

And please be upstanding when I inform you that for a limited time only, and for the right price of course, you too can claim yourself a big fat slice of this incredible arachnid action!

Find a loving surprise in each of her eyes! Crawl on in to her sultry web of sin! Claim safe harbour down in her parlour!

YOU KNOW YOU WANT TO!

So come, play hidey with the spidey! Spend just one hour with this spindly saucepot and you will sample some of the sickest pleasures this side of the underworld. And remember friends: if you make it out alive, you get half your money back...

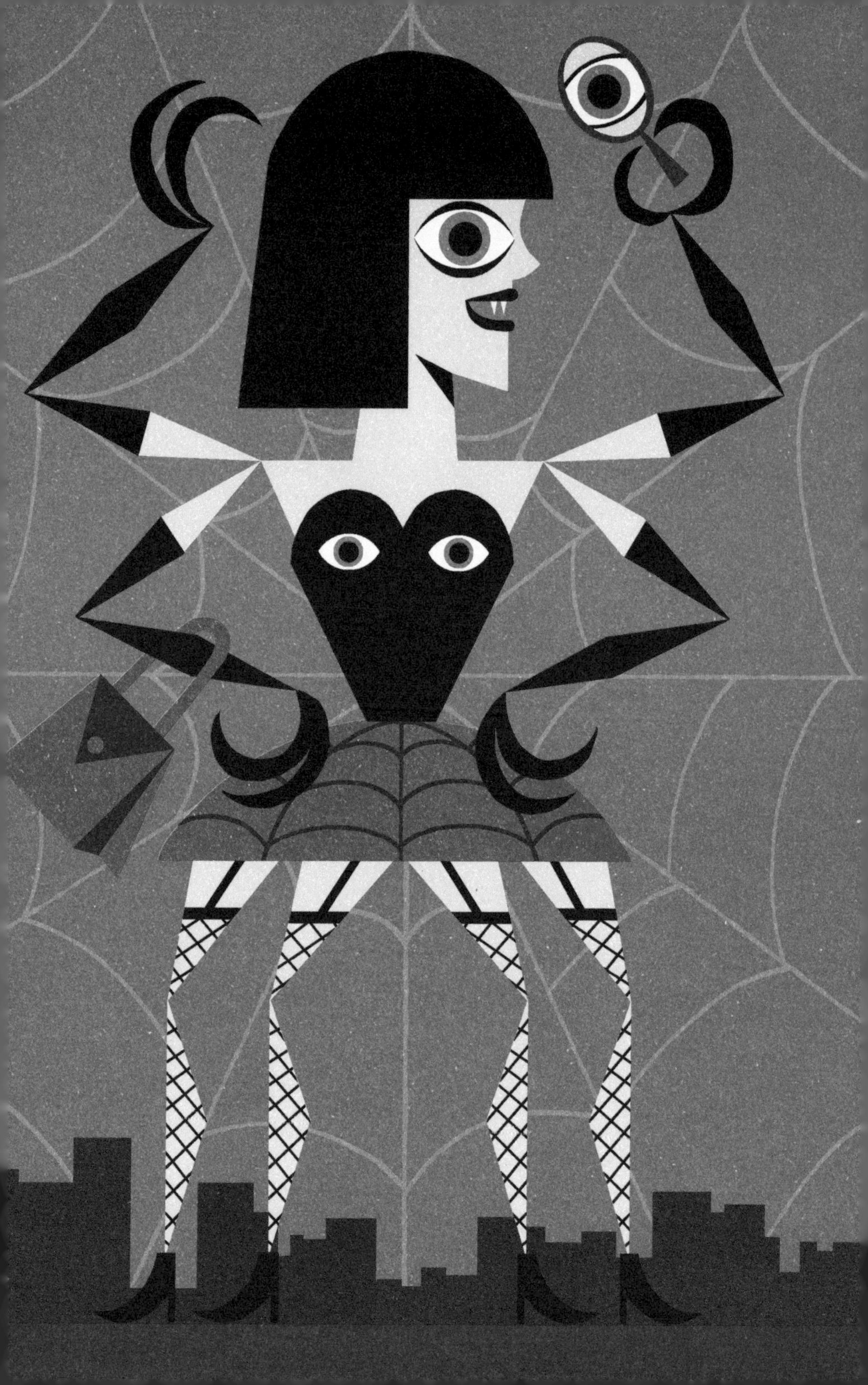

WANYŬDŎ

Ho! Stop peasant! I demand assistance! Come now, hurry, before my fiery-face extinguishes. How dare thee walk, insolent pig-dung? RUN! I am thy Daimyo, Lord of this land, and thou ought do as I say gladly or suffer dire consequences, rollicking scum-beetle!

Oh fear not my travelling wheel, nor flaming visage, thou shalt not be harmed. I would merely have thee as my companion, wretched commoner, despite thine physical hilarities. So, pray, travel by mine side. But hurry do, thou disguster of children, and give shove lest I topple!

Will thou stagger with me a while toward the gates of Hell? I am the Keeper of Keys after all. Oh blubber not thou hideous chub! Surely thou dost not think I should require a soul so cheap as thine? The very thought sets mine own flames aquiver...

Ah, at last we arrive! Surely thou could not travel such a distance without sneaking but a peek at the Devil's unholy barbeque?

Good. Now, slope a little closer. No no, 'tis anything but dangerous. Go forth: poke that bulbous bonce of yours inside. Get a good gander.

I swear, thou shalt remain safe.
That's right, I have thee...

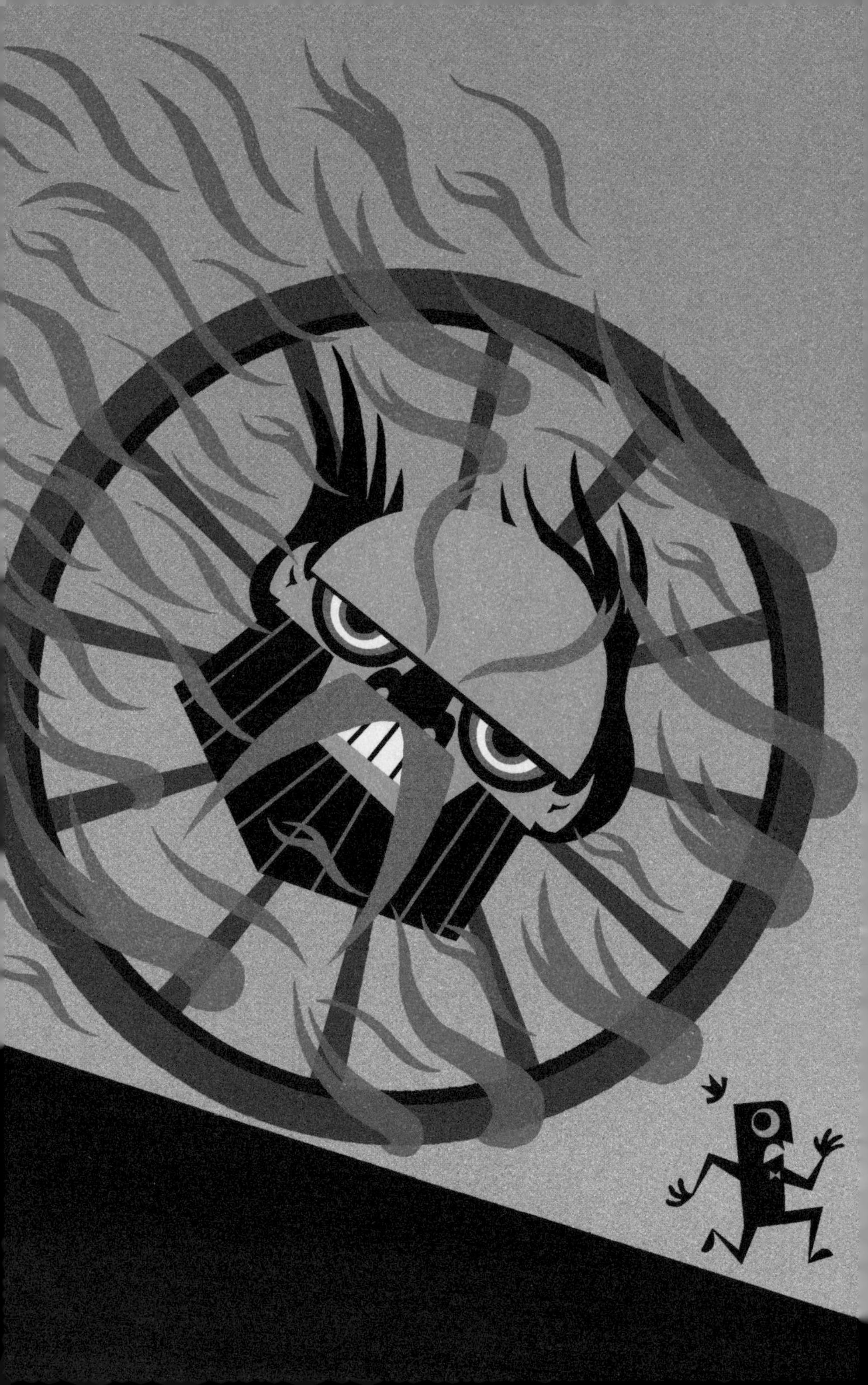

DATEOTOKO FISHU SAN

*It's embarrassing having to drive
myself home after a party.*

*I like to go out but it's no
fun going alone.*

*There's nothing wrong with
wearing a cocktail dress to bed.*

Sound familiar? Do not feel ashamed. Why should you not want to have a good time? You have earned it! Whatever the reason, if someone does not take proper care of you, then it's high time you did something about it. That's what I'm here for.

If you're in need of attention, but discretion is the problem, perhaps I can be your solution. Call now, and book a date with Dateotoko Fishu San.

This dapper dandy rules supreme in the competitive world of Escort Services, and with over Six Hundred years experience, I'm still as 'fresh' as ever. So forget about sleeping! Put that dress on and I will show you good times.

Dateotoko Fishu San respects you.
But do you respect yourself
enough, to let him?

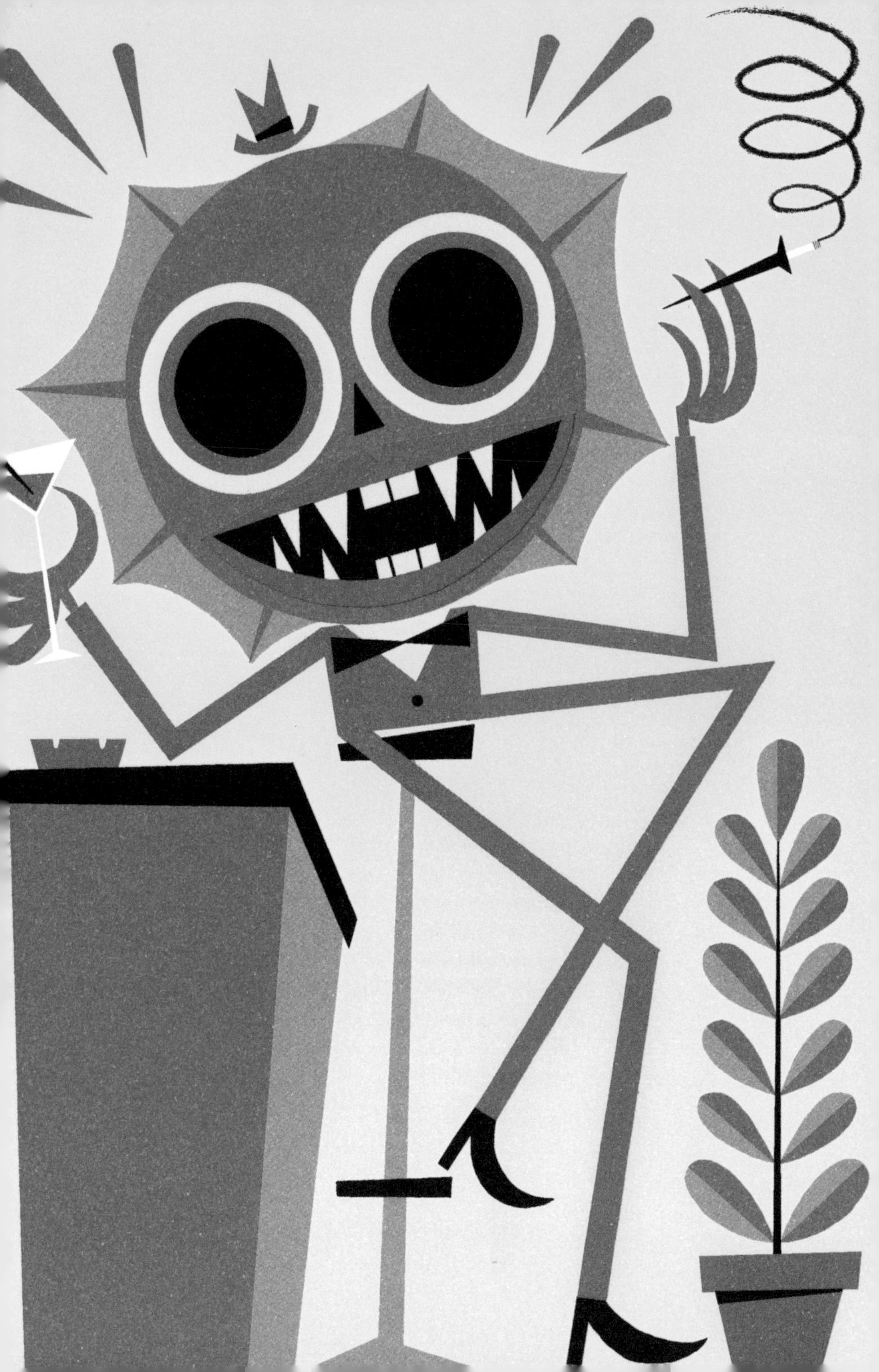

AMIKIRI

For many years now, Amikiri has provided a hearty challenge to many a young hunter wanting to test their mettle, but to date not one has even come close to supping on the exotic flesh trapped within that alluring exoskeleton. For not only is Amikiri well protected, but she is also battle-ready, gifted as she is with the triple threat of two terrible claws and one honking great beak.

Any would-be captors should also bear in mind that this creature is no slouch — she has been spotted all over town, snipping fishing nets down to stocking size with those stylish pincers of hers. Some believe she does this to evade capture, while others feel she is merely protecting her right to dress as she pleases. Most likely, it is a combination of the two.

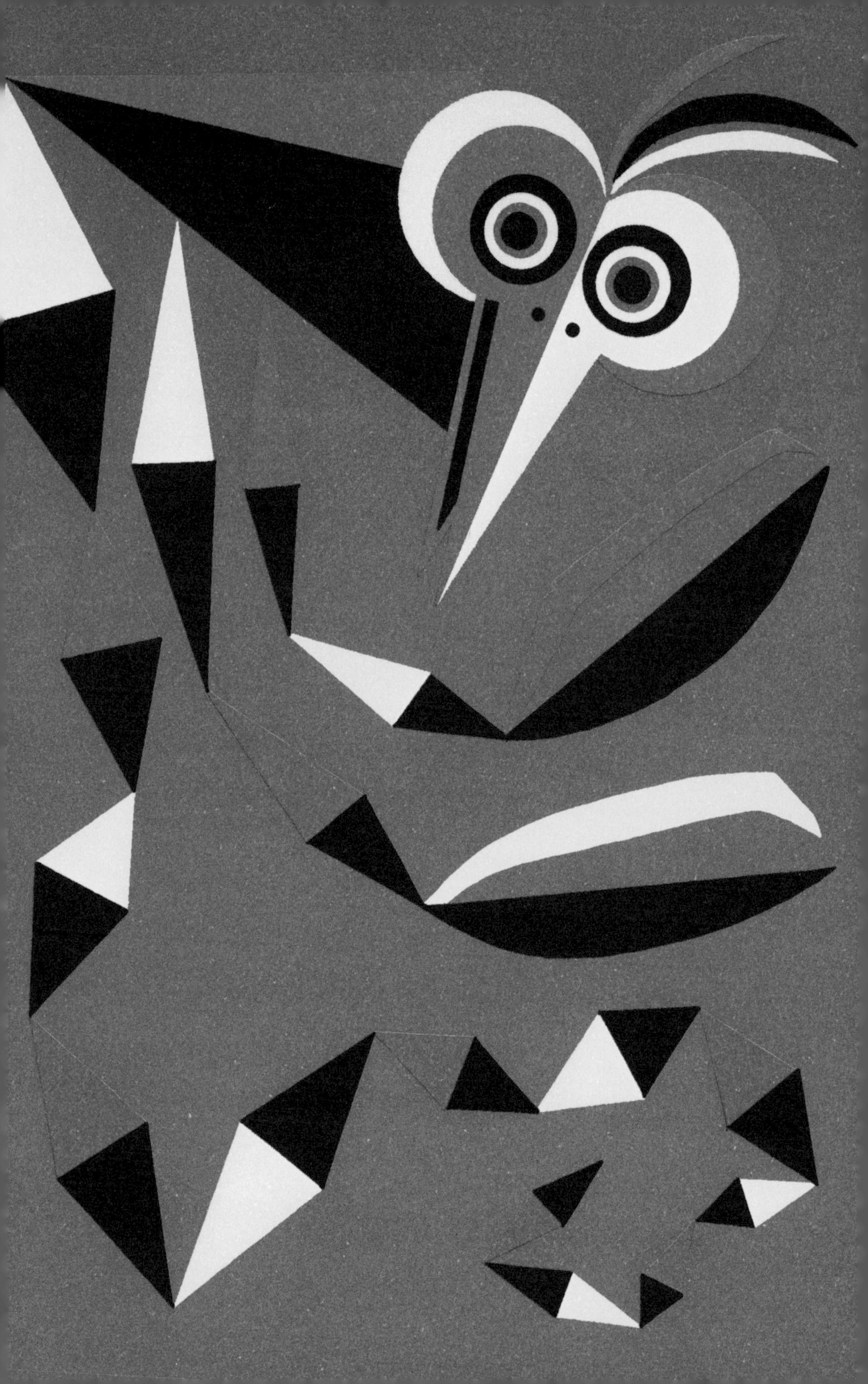

INUGAMI

Possess many enemies, but lack the wherewithal to slaughter them yourself?

JUST ASK INUGAMI

Cannot stand noisy eaters, but lack the throat crushing strength required to teach those monsters the lessons they deserve?

JUST ASK INUGAMI

Imbeciles make you want to rip your own heart out? And smack them to death with it?? But you just can't be bothered???

JUST ASK INUGAMI

Truth: this loyalist dog-beast can dispose of all troublemakers in the wag of a tail. You dream the punishment. He dishes it out. Hassle free horror from the comfort of your own home and at low-low prices.

No assembly required. Your INUGAMI arrives prestarved, beheaded and cursed, all ready for remote controlled carnage. So stay home my friend, eat rice cakes and peanut butter, and worry no more about those treacherous scum.

YOU relax. WE will take care of business.

INUGAMI TAKES CARE OF BUSINESS

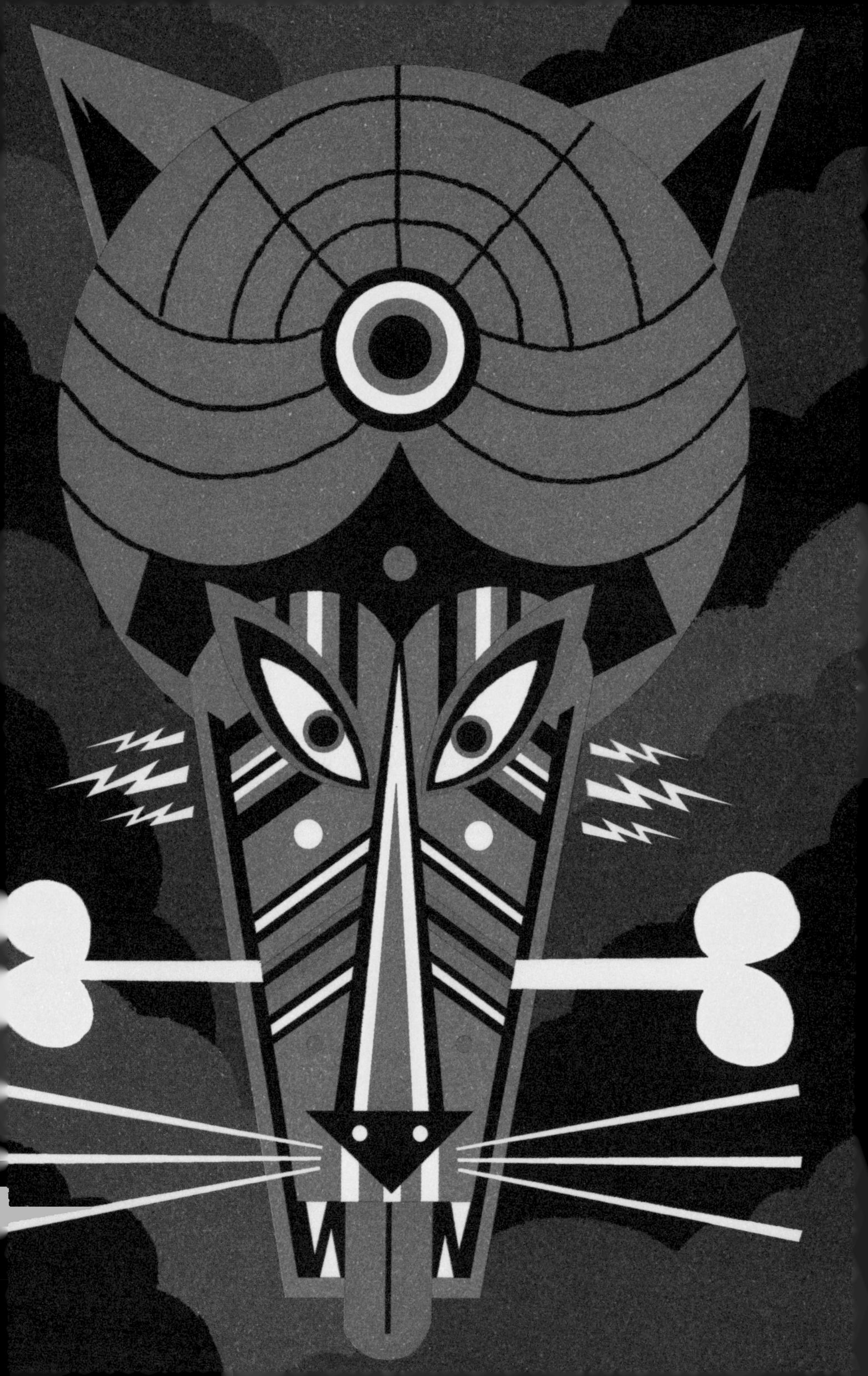

HAKUTAKU

Hakutaku is the diamond in the rough of all our lives. **HE** is a beautiful, shining example of everything we hold dear, and we love **HER** greatly. Hakutaku provides for us. **HE** makes our meals and drives us to work and tucks us in at night because **SHE** loves us as much as we love **IT.**

Hakutaku sees into the future and warns us of what's to come, to protect us and to shield us from the unending horrors of this world.

Hakutaku protects our unborn babes, brings us luck, inspires us to do great work, and all of this is done not for gain, but for love.

Hakutaku is all things to all men, and maybe more. Feel **HIS** warmth. Bask in **HER** glory. Stroke **IT'S** beard.

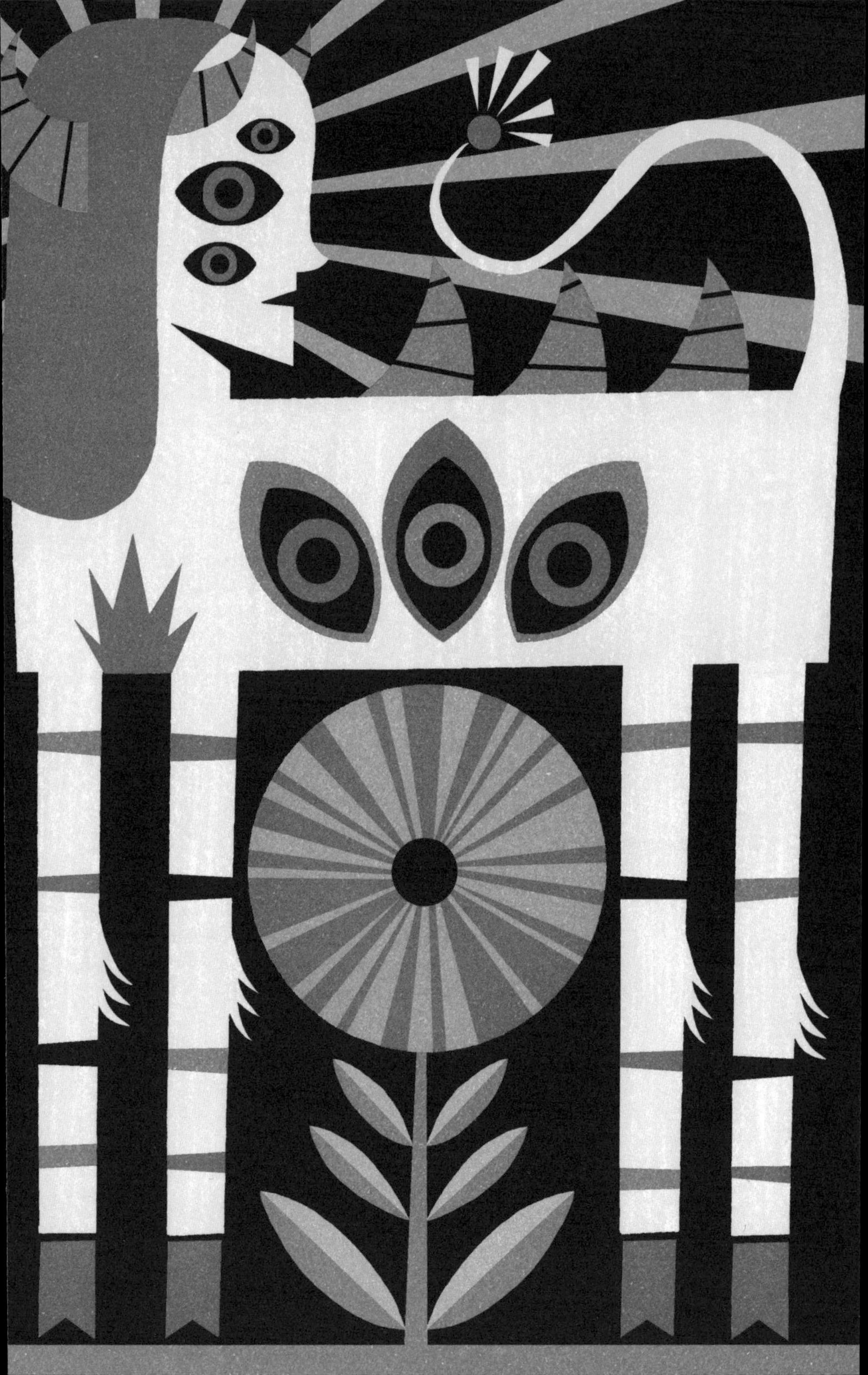

NUE

A treasure trove of tantalising tastiness,
Nue laughs defiantly at all pitiful attempts
to define its greatness. Try to imagine, if
you can, a being so wonderful as to possess
features such as

The HEAD of a proud Monkey!
The BODY of a most gullible Tanuki!
The LIMBS of a fierce fighting Tiger!
A TAIL comprised of a writhing wriggling Serpent!
And the VOICE of a delicate twittering Thrush!

And yet, despite being 98% super-magic,
sightings of Nue are still considered by many
to be an omen of grave misfortune, which
has lead to his lifetime banning from both
Farmers' Markets and Children's Hospitals.

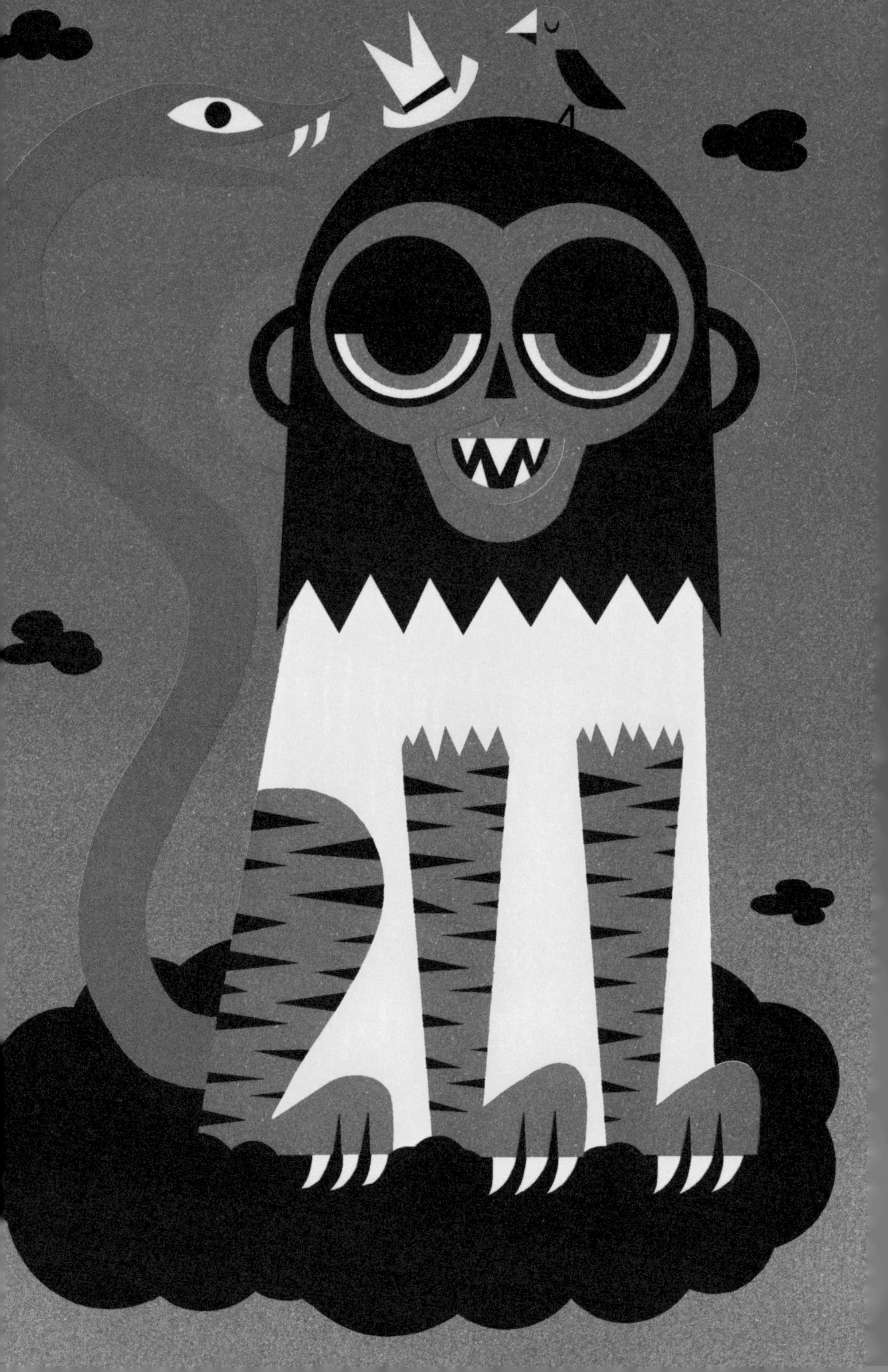

NURE-ONNA

My Dearest, I write to you with tears in my eyes, and love in my heart. Beautiful Nure-Onna, I am your servant. Do with me as you will, but I beg you, do not send me away, for it would be too much to bear.

You told me that I should be afraid, that I should actually fear you, but I do not. I cannot. I pray you do not take me for a fool; I know the tales people tell. I have heard much of forests destroyed by your whipping tail, of children threatened by vampiric fangs into eating their vegetables, of blood feasts, of carnal lust...

Well my deadly darling, I see the lie. Every word I hear against you is a dagger in my heart. I would gladly strike down all who speak ill of you, but I must not begin on that path, for, I know, it may prove to be without end. I beg you, perfect Nure-Onna, let me comfort you when their words pierce your tender heart. Let me be your companion on your punishing quest for peaceful times. Most of all, my poisonous princess, let yourself accept my love.

I dream that some day I will once again wash your hair by the riverside.

xxxxx

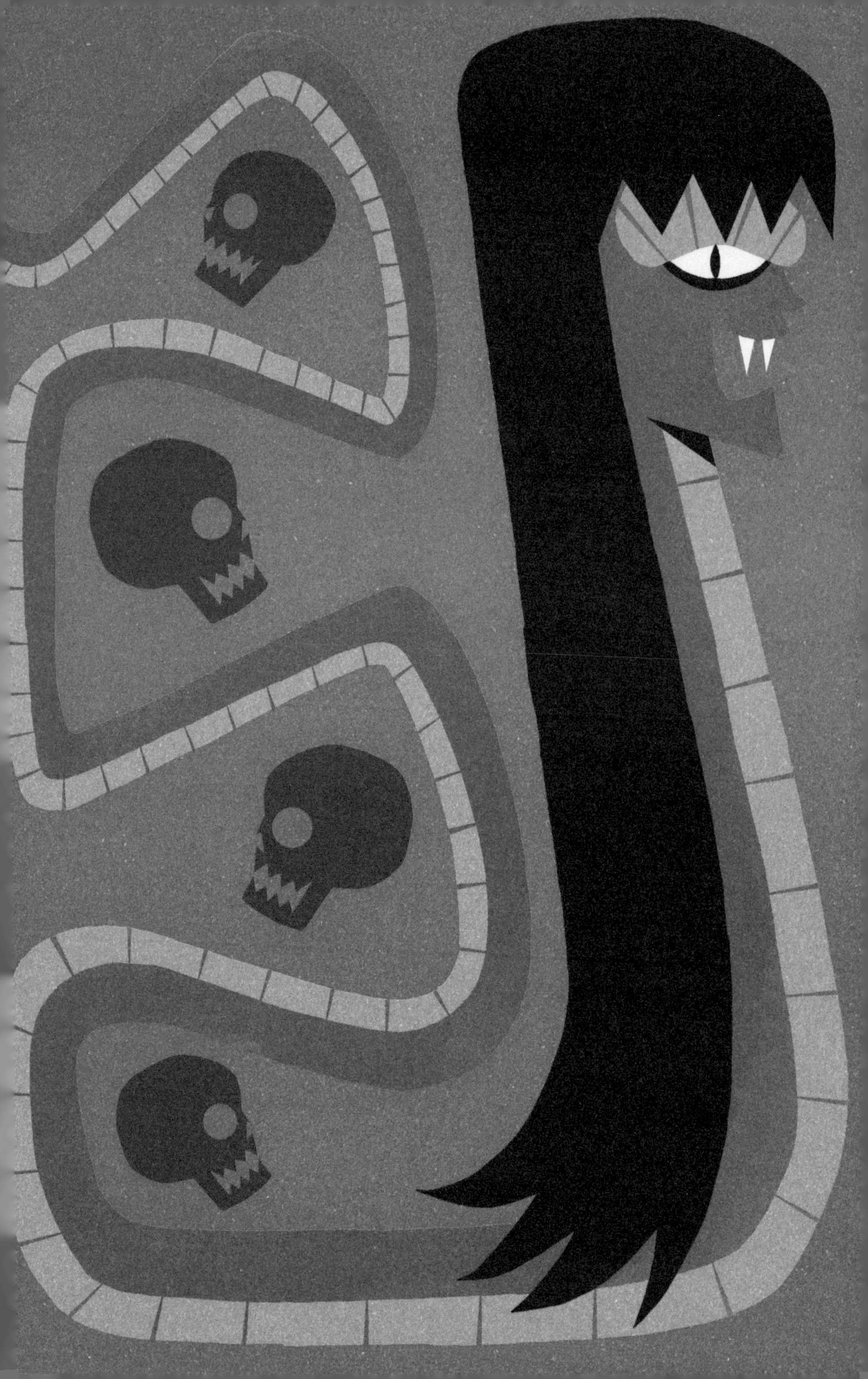

SONG OF THE
KAPPA

Oh, a tasty human child
is what I want for tea!
My tummy rumbles as I swim upstream,
when I spy you beneath a tree.

My webbed toes splash softly,
and my scaly skin's well hid.
There's no way you'll see me in this stream.
until a cry from that other kid...

Shouts 'Li-Po, what do you know?
It looks like you've got a bite!'
But fast as a flash, you trade smile for scream
when my shell comes into light.

'Fear not little snack!'
I call out to you in earnest.
'There's nothing to fear but the sweetest of dreams,
so lie down, and take a rest.'

'Troublemaker!' you cry.
'Bass Kimono-peeper!
Breaker of wind! Taker of life!
Not bream, nor squid, but reaper!'

'Hush now tasty morsel,
I must prepare the feast!
Do you really expect to thwart my schemes
by behaving like a beast?'

'I'll quick fry your eyes,
and slow roast those legs-
you'll taste tip-top super-sweet supreme!
So come child, don't make me beg.'

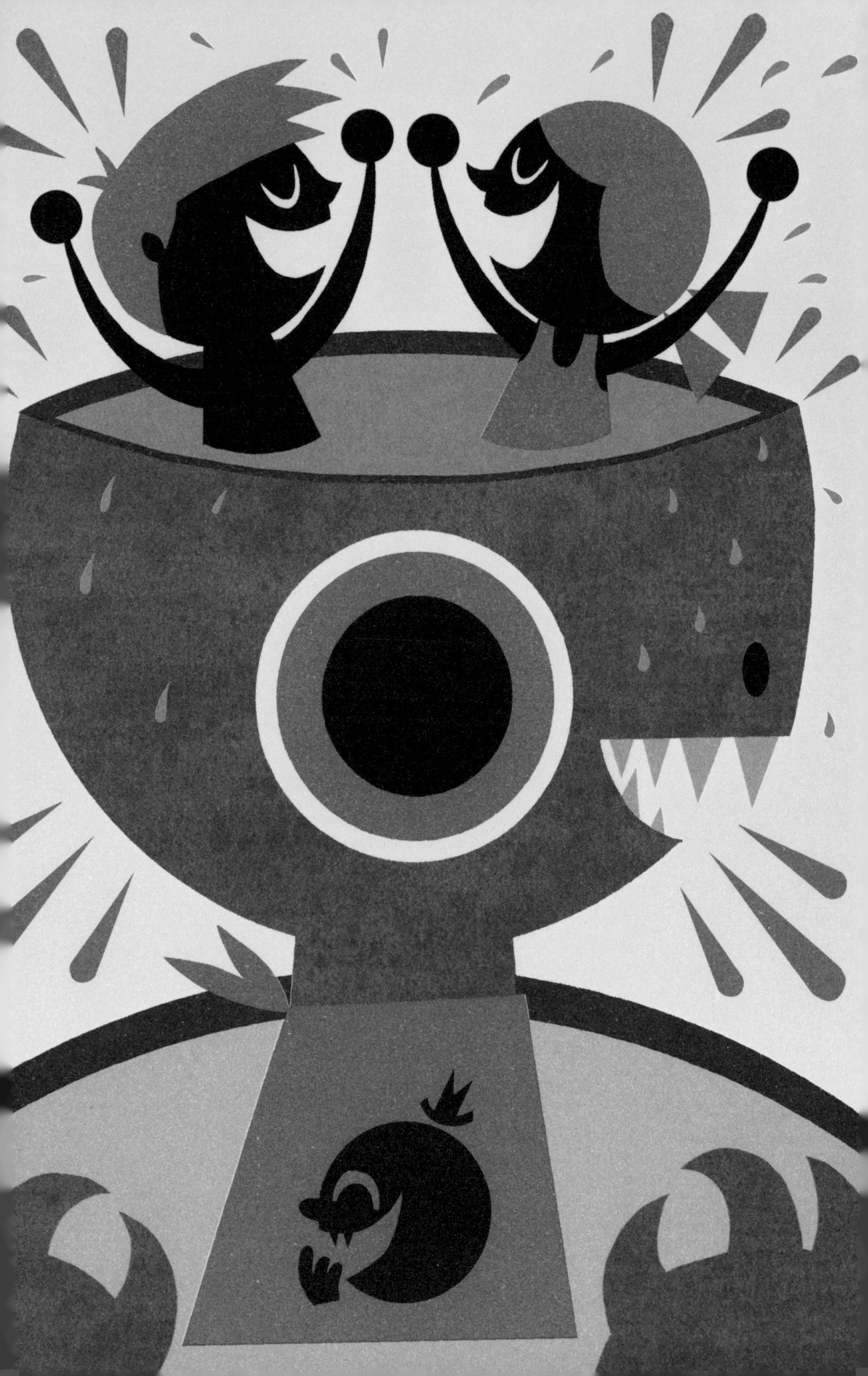

KONAKI-JIJI

Once upon a time a brave and powerful warrior was travelling home from battle when he was struck by a terrible sound; somewhere in the distance, the forlorn wail of an infant cried out to him. Searching as bravely as he could, it did not take long before he did indeed find a swaddled mass, its no-doubt cherubic face smeared with muck and dirt. Valiantly our prince lifted the bundle to his mighty chest and, without regard for his own safety, began foraging for berries with which to feed his ward.

Alas, our plucky champion might have studied the little creature more closely for quickly it began to grow. And very soon, it was so heavy that our hero's courageous legs did begin to buckle. The brave and powerful warrior turned to reassure the sweet stray in his arms that it had nothing to fear, that he would protect the helpless soul even if it should mean his very life! But of course, his life was already lost. For this was no ordinary foundling. No, this was the Konaki-Jiji! An ancient shape-shifting alcoholic, this beast would con its way into some would-be protectors arms, before expanding its girth to such a disgusting extent as to crush his victim to death!

And so it went with our bold and daring champion. Squished by a giant baby, who stole his purse, and then got plastered.

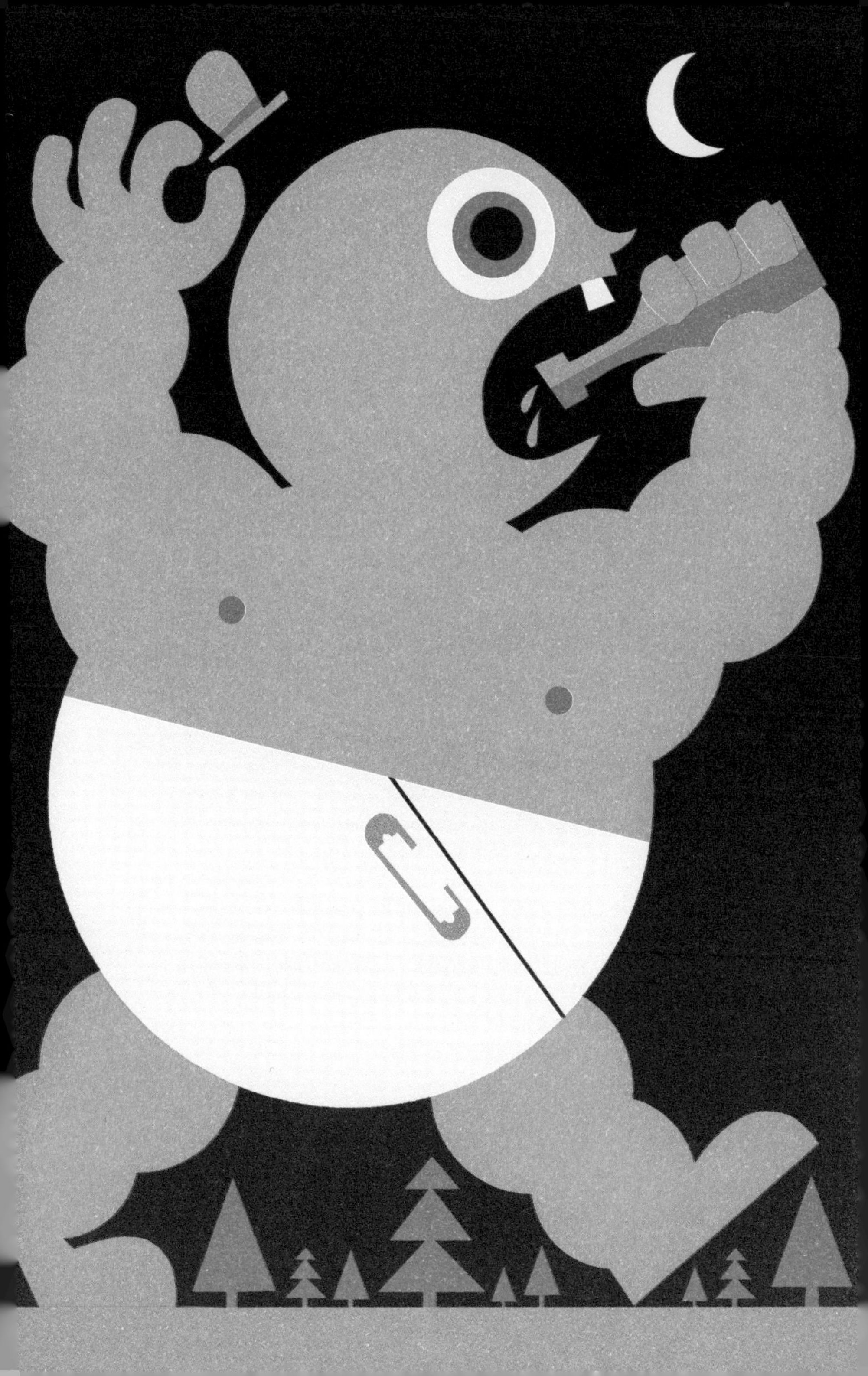

TAIMATSU MARU

Come no closer for it is true - I am the Drummer of Death! Wherever I lead, foolish men will follow; into hardship, into misery, into pain. This is my path, and I suggest you do not cross it.

So go! Be away, and trouble me no more, for I am on holiday! It's a city-break actually, quite nice so far, despite your puny brethren pointing their flash-boxes at me as they scream in disbelief. If they are so scared, then why do they keep coming? I am not a rollercoaster – I am Taimatsu Maru!

Where I once was the Harbinger of Doom, now I have become the Tourist of Terror! I shall scratch out your every flea-market, hunt down your greatest bargains, and purchase relentlessly in your so-called Super Stores.

So! Fall to your knees in frustration as I jump the queue for your multiplex. Shriek in admiration as I traverse your longest, most bendy waterslides. And rub your greedy paws together as I empty my enormous purse into your seediest, most overpriced discothèques. This is exciting!

Now, flee if you want to live.
But stay, if you wish to party...

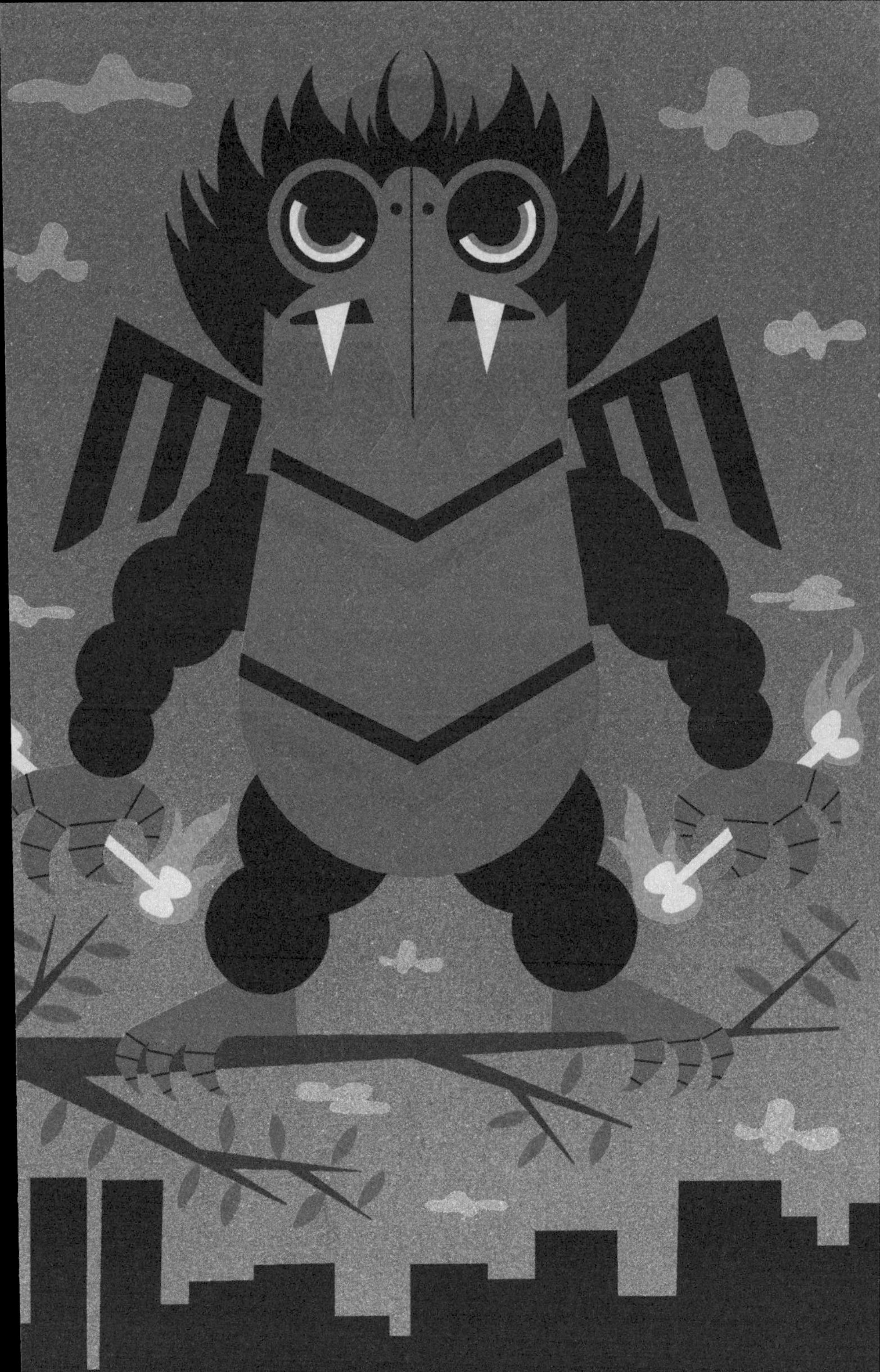

BEN NEWMAN

Newman floundered around in the dross pits of earth for several millennia before finally gluing his brain blocks together, gettin' up and goin' home. Since then he's been honing his haughty enigma status in schools and small taverns across the countryside, and fitting himself into awkward spaces. His favourite food is pi.

SCOTT DONALDSON

Donaldson was a struggling pupil at the school of clean-shaven men when he became a werewolf. This only made matters worse. He became a terrible dilettante and showed his fur all over town. Rehabilitated, he now he lives in the country where he teaches werewolf young to read. He eats mostly mutton.

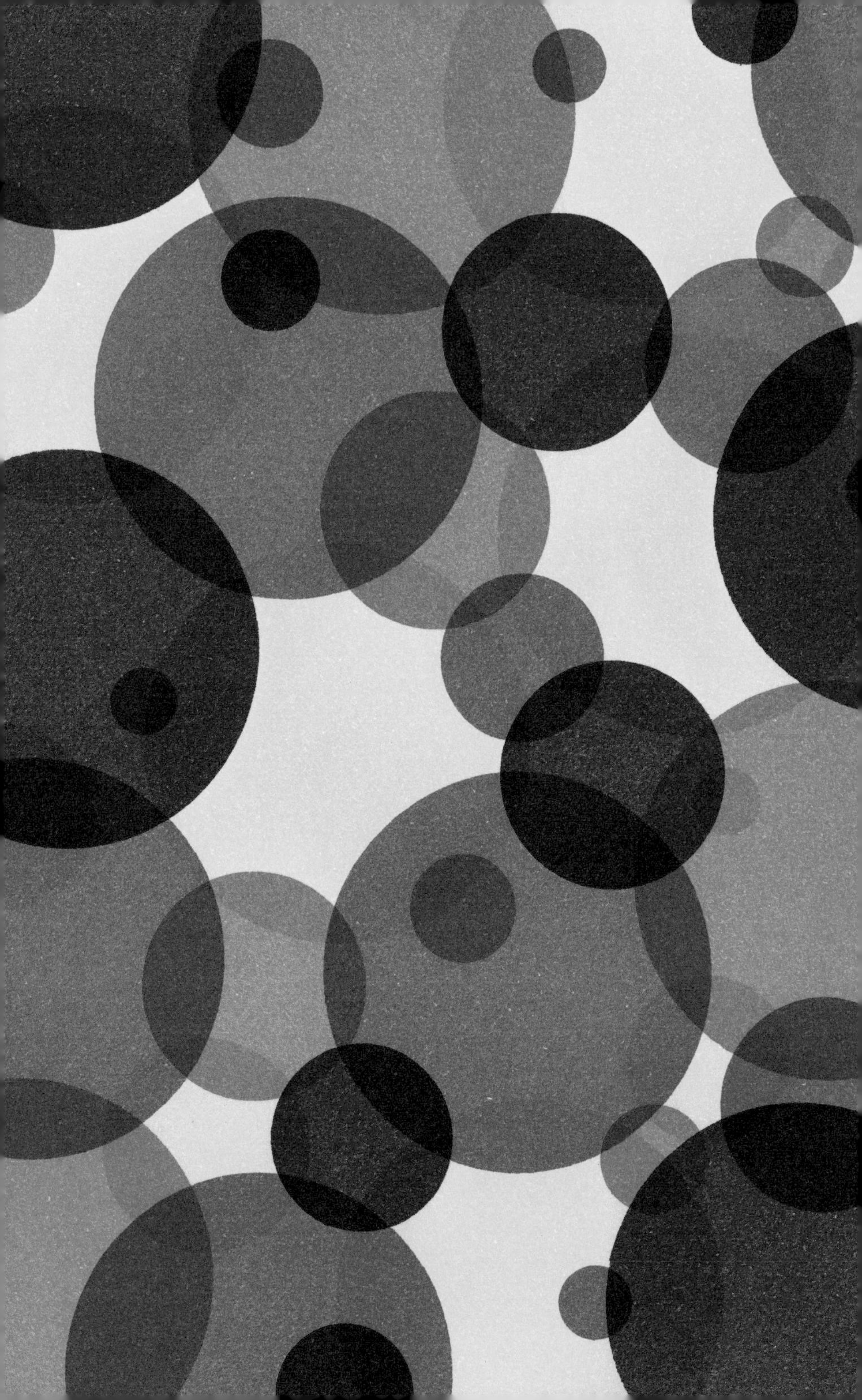